Endorsements

"Content with a mediocre business? If so, don't read Joel's book. If, however, you are interested in maximizing corporate value—both today and at sale time—then I highly recommend CEO to CVO. Joel has spent a lifetime helping CEOs become CVOs and has distilled the lessons learned into this practical and highly accessible playbook for creating 'Gotta Have' businesses."

—Brian Burt
Chair, Emerging Business Group Snell and Wilmer LLP

"In this exceptionally well-written book, Strom makes the powerful case that CEOs should see themselves as a Chief Value Officers (CVO). It shows the key areas CEOs should focus on to lead their companies to become 'Gotta Have' businesses. This is a must read for every CEO and business leader."

—Greg Miller
Managing Director, Alliance of CEOs

"The author's experience in both running and advising growing businesses makes him the perfect person to write this book. He takes a deep dive into what creates value in those businesses and why it must be the CEO's primary focus. Just as he shows that creating a 'Gotta Have' business increases enterprise value, this 'Gotta Have' book will add value to any CEO or owner of a growing business."

—Robert J. Strom, PhD
Former Director of Entrpreneurship Research
Ewing Marion Kauffman Foundation

"This book does a good job of thoroughly covering a topic important to all business owners and leaders in a way that makes it an enjoyable read. It presents a strong case for maximizing business value and for the things every CEO needs to be doing to make that happen but unfortunately often fail to focus on in their regular daily routine."

—Robert Hurst
Chairman
Phoenix Specialty Manufacturing Company

CEO TO CVO

CEO TO CVO
Moving Your Business from Ordinary to Extraordinary

Joel Strom

JONES MEDIA
PUBLISHING

CEO to CVO Moving Your Business from Ordinary to Extraordinary Copyright © 2020 by Joel Strom.

All rights reserved. No part of this publication may be reproduced, distributed, or transmitted in any form or by any means, including photocopying, recording, or other electronic or mechanical methods, without the prior written permission of the author, except in the case of brief quotations embodied in critical reviews and certain other noncommercial uses permitted by copyright law.

Disclaimer:

The author strives to be as accurate and complete as possible in the creation of this book, notwithstanding the fact that the author does not warrant or represent at any time that the contents within are accurate due to the rapidly changing nature of the Internet.

While all attempts have been made to verify information provided in this publication, the Author and the Publisher assume no responsibility and are not liable for errors, omissions, or contrary interpretation of the subject matter herein. The Author and Publisher hereby disclaim any liability, loss or damage incurred as a result of the application and utilization, whether directly or indirectly, of any information, suggestion, advice, or procedure in this book. Any perceived slights of specific persons, peoples, or organizations are unintentional.

In practical advice books, like anything else in life, there are no guarantees of income made. Readers are cautioned to rely on their own judgment about their individual circumstances to act accordingly. Readers are responsible for their own actions, choices, and results. This book is not intended for use as a source of legal, business, accounting or financial advice. All readers are advised to seek the services of competent professionals in legal, business, accounting, and finance field.

Printed in the United States of America

ISBN: 978-1-948382-09-0 paperback
JMP2020.5

DEDICATION

To the person who has had to endure my dreams, my optimism, my work schedules, and my general craziness but who has stood by me and encouraged me for over fifty years—the love of my life, my wife, my advisor, my editor, my best friend, and the best mother and Nana, June.

CONTENTS

Acknowledgments..1

Introduction..4

Chapter 1: CEO as CVO 15

Chapter 2: Strategic Value and the Four Pillars 26

Chapter 3: Why Its Always the Right Time 35

Chapter 4: Strategic Value Acceleration 50

Chapter 5: Pillar Number 1—Financial...........65

Chapter 6: Pillar Number 2—Strategic............77

Chapter 7: Pillar Number 3—Operational.......89

Chapter 8: Pillar Number 4—Industry 106

Chapter 9: The CVO in Family Business 116

Chapter 10: Leading as the CVO 124

Conclusion 138

About the Author 144

ACKNOWLEDGMENTS

The advice I always gave my sons, and will pass on to my grandkids as well, is that life is too short to not do what you really love and have a passion for. The many great CEOs and their companies that I've had the opportunity to work with over my career, have enabled me to do just that. I've unlimited respect and admiration for your entrepreneurial drive, your dedication, and your successes. I thank you all for believing in me and trusting me to help you create extraordinary businesses. There were often times when I felt like I was learning more from your collective wisdom than I was providing. Obviously, without you there wouldn't have been any content for this book.

I would be remis if I didn't also acknowledge the role that my numerous business partners had on my career and on the contents of this book. You lived many of the value-creation journeys with me.

I've been inspired in my personal journey by too many people to list here. Some in positive ways that encouraged me to go forward with my entrepreneurial drive and to continue on whenever I was knocked down. There were also some who, by telling me I would never accomplish what I set out to do, provided me the incentive I needed to prove them wrong. I thank them all and hope that in some way I've repaid the favor.

This acknowledgement wouldn't be complete without including my seven greatest fans: Asher, Ben, Hannah, Elliot, Gabby, Finley, and Viola. You're my true reward. You have all been my Chief Value Officers and created so much value in my life. You have enabled me to go from Ordinary to Extraordinary. I'm sure each one of you will be Extraordinary in whatever paths

Acknowledgments

you choose to take in your lives. Just have the passion and love what you do.

INTRODUCTION

> Don't be afraid to give up the good to go for the great
>
> John D. Rockefeller

It's All about Strategic Value

Imagine owning a great company. A company everyone wants. One that's truly valuable. Obviously not an Amazon or Apple, but your company. You can do it. It's not easy. It takes commitment and sacrifice, but it's within your reach. Others have done it and so can you.

This book is about doing just that. It's about taking on the role of CVO, or Chief Value Officer, and building a great company. It's about building a sustainable, exciting, innovative, fun,

Introduction

valuable company. A company that provides you with the rewards you have worked for and deserve. A company that provides you as its owner with options. A "Gotta Have" company that everyone wants.

It's about Strategic Value and the Four Pillars. Strategic Value is a concept and process to guide you. It has enabled CEO's to become CVO's and create extraordinary companies with extraordinary company value. Now you're probably asking what exactly is Strategic Value? By the time you're done with this book, my goal is that it becomes part of your day-to-day vocabulary.

So, what is Strategic Value and what makes it different than any other measure of business value? The concept of Strategic Value isn't only a theory, I developed it based on reality. The reality that there's much more that determines a company's value than simply a mathematical calculation involving the last three years' EBITDA, sales, or profits. A company's Strategic Value is created by the same factors that contribute to creating a great company. Strategic Value simply provides a concept and a tool to measure it and accomplish it.

Don't over think it. The Strategic Value concept is straight forward and logical. There are Four Pillars that support your company's Strategic Value: Financial, Strategic, Operational, and Industry. Within each of those pillars, there are various components that, depending on their strength, can create or reduce your Strategic Value. In the chapters ahead, we'll define each of the pillars and the components within them. Then you will learn a process that you can use to accelerate the Strategic Value of your business.

The Strategic Value concept is real and proven. I developed it from the experiences I've had and the realities I've seen over my long career in business. It started with my early career days in larger companies and with my ownership of a growing manufacturing company. The concept was truly honed during my years running consulting firms, helping

Introduction

privately held companies successfully grow and create value. It was proven when I was a partner in an investment banking firm selling privately held companies. It was then confirmed during my stint as the CEO of a technical product engineering and manufacturing company.

My goal in this book is to utilize those experiences and stories to help other leaders, like yourself, understand what can be accomplished. This book is intended to show how you can transition your business from ordinary to extraordinary. As the title of this book indicates, it's focused on what I believe should be your primary role as business owner or CEO: to be your company's Chief Value Officer. In that role your only responsibility is to maximize your company's Strategic Value. By doing that, you will accomplish much more than simply a maximum sale price at the time you eventually sell the business. As I will show, maximizing Strategic Value also means higher profitability, more owner options, and financial insurance for you and your family. I will prove to you my claim that **it's always the right time**

to be accelerating your company's Strategic Value.

Creating a "Gotta Have"

I will often refer to a "Gotta Have" business. This label refers to a business that has maximized its Strategic Value to become a business everyone wants. It's where you want to be even if you're not looking to sell. Being a "Gotta Have" says that you own the best. Who does not want to own the best?

Then, when you're ready to sell, your "Gotta Have" business stands out from the rest of the crowd and can truly increase the sale price beyond your expectations.

Leadership's Role

In writing this book about creating Strategic Value, I couldn't ignore the role that your leadership as the CEO/CVO or owner/CVO of your company plays in successfully accelerating Strategic Value. After spending the majority of my career helping my clients accelerate their company's Strategic Value, I had the opportunity

Introduction

to spend a few years as the CEO/CVO of a client's company. During that time, sitting in that leadership seat, I was able to reconfirm the concept of Strategic Value and the results it creates for a company. I also confirmed the role that the CEO/CVO's leadership plays in the success of the process. I've devoted an entire chapter to those leadership confirmations.

My Story

I've spent most of my career helping CEOs become successful CVOs. I started my practice after selling a manufacturing company. A company that I had bought when I was too young and inexperienced. Believing in myself and thinking I knew a lot more about growing a business than I did, I bought it. I took the risk and made the bet. That experience taught me, sometimes the hard way, a lot of what works and, unfortunately, what doesn't in running a business and growing its value. I learned lessons that set the stage for my career and eventually for the basis of this book.

I bought that company when I realized that I wasn't cut out for corporate life and for being told what to do and where to live. I needed control of my life and I needed to have something that I could, have true ownership in. I gave up my regular paycheck and purchased that company. Then, like many of you have experienced, the reality of what I'd done hit me. The change from employee to owner was overwhelming, but it was exciting. Suddenly, every decision was an important one and could have a profound effect on me, the company, my employees, and my family. A scary feeling but a great feeling, a feeling of ownership and of control.

The idea to do consulting for other CEOs on growth and value creation was initially just something to do after getting out of the manufacturing business. "I'll do this 'til I find my next thing," I told myself. Then I realized I really loved doing what I was doing. I created a consulting firm and before I knew it, over thirty years had gone by. Over a recent five-year period, I left consulting to take advantage

Introduction

of a great opportunity. I took a position as the CEO for a client company and performed the role of CEO/CVO full time. Now I'm back doing the one thing that I love the most, helping companies accelerate their Strategic Value, create "Gotta Have" businesses, and maximize their enterprise value.

During all these years, I've worked with and been involved in more companies than I can count. I've witnessed some great success stories where owners and their families have become multimillionaires by creating great Strategic Value and "Gotta Have" businesses. I've also witnessed disappointments when working with businesses that had great potential but whose leadership didn't have the commitment or dedication to reach that potential. I share many of those real-life stories in this book to illustrate the CVO and Strategic Value concepts and the great power it has to create "Gotta Have" businesses. They're true stories, but I've changed names and sometimes industries to protect their privacy.

The journey to write this book has been something I've thought about many times in the past but never had the time to embark on. Now I've the luxury of time, and the good news is that I've more years of experience and even more importantly, many more stories to tell.

I believe that one can never stop learning. That no matter how old you are and what experiences you have had, there's always something new to see and learn and even marvel at. Every time I think I've seen it all, I see something new. In my recent time as CEO/CVO, I realized again that there are always new ideas and thoughts to learn about and apply. I learned firsthand that what I told my clients for years was correct. We should never stop seeking and using advice from people outside our companies who may see things from a different perspective. As CEO/CVO, I never hesitated to bring in consultants to help in our journey to create a great company. Despite my experience and age, I joined a CEO peer group. I'm sure I was the oldest member of the group (by quite a bit), but our meeting day

Introduction

was one of my favorite days of the month. I learned from every (younger) member of the group. I also encouraged (and paid for) my leadership team and others in the company to take advantage of any opportunity to learn and improve themselves. We brought in people from other companies to learn how other companies operated. We had team members from different areas of the company presenting to their peers at "lunch and learns." It's in that vein that I write this book. New ideas and perspectives that you and your team can use in your quest to create your "Gotta Have" business—a business that everyone wants.

Stories and Examples

I use many stories to illustrate how Strategic Value works to create "Gotta Have" businesses. These are all true stories. I've changed the names of these companies and their owners to protect their privacy.

Strategic Value Assessment

One way to get even more value from this book is to utilize my free online CVO Strategic

Value Assessment tool. You can do it either before or after reading the book. The assessment will ask you questions about your company relating to the components of the Four Pillars of Strategic Value. Once completed, you will receive your company's current Strategic Value Score and suggestions on how to improve it. Once you have received your score, should you desire, you can schedule a personal, no cost or obligation discussion with me to review your score and help you begin your Strategic Value-acceleration journey.

You can access the assessment and request your personal session at www.ChiefValueOfficers.com.

CHAPTER 1: CEO AS CVO

> If you really look closely, most overnight successes took a long time.
>
> Steve Jobs

From Growth to Growth Management to Value Creation

I'm starting this book with a great story. It's a story with a very happy ending: the founder, his family, and their company's CEO became very wealthy. It's also the story that brought the concept of Strategic Value, the CVO, and the "Gotta Have" business into perspective for me.

When we first started working with Waterborne Industries (name changed to protect privacy), my firm provided what we referred to as Growth Management advisory services. These companies were in just about every industry, from manufacturers to distributors to retailers and even large law practices and funeral homes. Growth Management was a method of helping companies successfully grow from smaller entrepreneurial businesses to what we referred to as "real" businesses. Most of our clients weren't struggling with getting sales. In fact, it was just the opposite. They were struggling to manage the growth created by those sales. Some were on the verge of growing themselves out of business. We focused on the infrastructure of those companies and what we termed the "infrastructure gaps" caused by growing sales faster than the company could support them. We helped our clients identify symptoms of support gaps, find the root cause, and fix them. Then we would work with them to develop plans to avoid future infrastructure support gaps.

Chapter 1: CEO as CVO

I was excited to work with Waterborne. They were a growing company in an exciting industry, but they were beginning to encounter support gap symptoms. It was a family-owned business. The founder admitted something few others do. He understood that he didn't have the desire or skill to lead their company to their goal. The plan was to grow from their current $15 million revenue to $100 million annual revenue in ten years, and then sell the company.

They brought in a young, nonfamily CEO to lead the company. My firm and I worked with them for nearly ten years until they were just short of their $100 million revenue goal. Larger companies in their same industry took notice. They had been watching this company's success, and just shy of their ten-year timeframe, they started getting offers to purchase the company. Despite being just short of their goal, the family decided to entertain those offers. After several offers and counter offers from numerous companies, all of whom saw potentially huge accretive benefits to buying the company, it was sold. Ownership had their choice of buyers and sold the company to one of them for over fifteen times EBITDA (earnings before interest, taxes, depreciation, and amortization). The sale nearly doubled what was the rule-of-thumb multiple valuation for their industry.

It was then that I realized that rule-of-thumb multiples for company value can be more than just nudged higher, they can be totally thrown out. If the company is what I now call a "Gotta Have" business, the value will be based on much more than simply the last three year's EBITDA. In this case, the eventual buyer and the other bidders knew that this wasn't just another acquisition. They knew that they would not only get a nice annual EBITDA but a great company that would provide them an advantage over their competition. They saw my client as a company that they had to have at nearly any price. It was truly a "Gotta Have."

Creating a "Gotta Have"

Let's go back and see what created the "Gotta Have" label. Over the years as Waterborne grew, leadership stayed focused on what was

Chapter 1: CEO as CVO

necessary to achieve and support that growth. The results included a very strong leadership team and systems being implemented that helped their efficiencies and customer service. Investments were made in new specialized equipment to improve margins and quality. A true outside advisory board was created and a strong culture of innovation for new products was built. But ownership and the CEO did one thing that made me realize what was most important to increasing value. This realization led to my transition from Growth Management to Strategic Value and to the need for the CEO to become the CVO. That one thing was to change their perspective. **To change it from a total focus on profit today to a focus of building value for tomorrow.**

Before you think it or have a panic attack, I'll ease your mind. Yes, you do need to make a profit today. However, having an exclusive focus on making profit and taking cash out today will prevent you from being able to make rational decisions regarding investment in the future of the company. Investing in infrastructure, talent, product development, technology, and even culture is the only way to create the sustainability, differentiation, and "Gotta Have" company that will accelerate your company value.

Sure, there's risk involved. You're placing bets on the future and some bets will be wrong. Waterborne, with its innovation culture, brought out a new product in a different market. It didn't work. The market didn't accept the new product and sales never took off. They made a big bet and they lost. They took it off the market but that didn't deter them from continuing to make big bets and from doing whatever they felt would be necessary to achieve their vision and accelerate their value.

To take the CVO title seriously, you need the stomach and patience to follow through with the commitment to accelerate company value. That means committing to making investments in the future of your company, often at the expense of today's profitability and cash flow. It means placing bets on future growth. It means you and your leadership team having confidence

Chapter 1: CEO as CVO

in your decisions, making those decisions, and continually measuring the results of those decisions.

This ability to focus and invest in the future is one of the advantages of owning a privately held company, because you, not Wall Street, make the rules. Public companies are often so driven by quarterly results that they sacrifice future success. Robert Iger, CEO of Disney, was a good example of someone who knew his primary role as CEO was to be the CVO. In one situation, knowing he was right, he ignored the profit-now mandate and made the decision in 2019 to go forward with Disney's own streaming service, Disney+. In doing so, he would give up current income for Disney content from other streaming services like Netflix. He exchanged it for the potential future success and corporate value to be had from controlling both the content and the delivery. It was his vision for the future of Disney.

In his book *The Ride of a Lifetime: Lessons Learned from 15 Years as CEO of the Walt Disney Company*, Iger (2019) states, "The decision to disrupt businesses that are fundamentally working but whose future is in question—intentionally taking on short-term losses in the hope of generating long-term growth—requires no small amount of courage."

As Iger stated, as CVO you need to have courage. Jeff Bezos is another leader known for courage. A time he showed that courage dates to 2004. At that time Amazon was smaller than eBay. Shipping took up to a week and customers were charged $9.48 for the service unless their order was over $25. An engineer at Amazon suggested a new concept and Bezos approved it. Prime Membership was born. For $79 per year you got free two-day shipping. Today, Prime is $119 per year and offers more perks. There are currently 150 million Prime subscribers, who are Amazon's most loyal customers. It obviously paid off, but it was a risk. As Bezos (2004) wrote at the time on Amazon's website, "We expect Amazon Prime to be expensive for

Chapter 1: CEO as CVO

Amazon.com in the short term. In the long term we hope to earn even more of your business, which will make it good for us too." He invested in the future and it proved to be a really good bet.

Vision and Commitment

Both Waterborne and Disney were focused on a vision. They both had painted a picture of what they wanted their future to look like. That vision drove their actions. Lots of companies paint the picture of their future, but few attain it. Why is that? It's commitment or the lack of it. The ones that do achieve their vision have the commitment to do what's necessary to get there. The vision of maximizing value and reaching $100 million in ten years was achieved because ownership focused on what was necessary to build long-term value, not on escalating current profit and taking cash out. There were times when ownership became weary, but they remained committed. Their patience paid off for them, for management, and for their employees. They waited for and received the bigger prize. There was little confusion or conflict in the company. The leadership team and the entire company knew the vision and understood the commitment. Everyone was in the boat and rowing in the same direction.

Strategic Value

I'm not alone in my contention that there is much more to creating value in a company than simply the bottom line. There are so many examples of the most valuable "Gotta Have" companies being just great companies. They're well run, efficient, innovative, growing, fun, and profitable. They stand out among their rivals. I developed the Strategic Value concept to give CVOs a straightforward tool and process to build valuable "Gotta Have" companies. Utilizing the Four Pillars of Strategic Value provides you—as the CVO—a methodology to engage everyone in creating a great company.

The concept of Strategic Value and the Four Pillars is defined in detail in chapter 2. Chapters 5-8 dig deeper into the components of the Four Pillars. Just to reiterate it again, Strategic Value is not only important when you're selling

Chapter 1: CEO as CVO

your business. In chapter 3 you will learn why it doesn't matter where in your business life cycle you are. Whether your plan is to exit your business in four years, four decades, or never, it's always the right time to be accelerating Strategic Value.

CHAPTER 2: STRATEGIC VALUE AND THE FOUR PILLARS

Be so good they can't ignore you.

Steve Martin

Company Value Comes from Much More Than Just Today's Profit

In the first chapter I shared a story with a happy ending and a family becoming very wealthy. Well here's another one. It goes down a different path, but it also has a very happy ending. This one stars a guy named Ted.

Chapter 2: Strategic Value and the Four Pillars

I knew Ted from college. He was a brilliant engineer and had started his company, Faraday Industries (name changed to protect privacy), right after graduation. They designed and built highly complex products for various industries. He and I lost touch over the years as he grew his company and I grew my consulting practice. Then his attorney reconnected us. Ted's company had grown but not to the extent it could've, and like most growing businesses it had gone through some rough patches. Once we reconnected, Ted wanted me to help him on some specific projects. As I got to know his company, I wasn't surprised to see how innovative his products were. I also identified some major infrastructure issues and support gaps that were negatively affecting his Strategic Value. "Yeah, yeah," he would tell me as I pushed him to address those issues, "we will get to them, but I've important product and customer priorities right now."

Then one day my phone rang. It was Ted. He was calling to tell me that he was approached by a group that was interested in buying Faraday Industries. The number they had initially thrown out to him was $25 million. Ted, although not actively pursuing a sale, had thought about selling and this was just too good to pass up. He made the decision to go forward with them. Then the buyers began their due diligence process. Once that was completed, we met them in Ted's conference room. We knew there were some Strategic Value issues that hadn't been addressed, so we expected some deductions from the $25 million initial offer. Ted's shock came when the potential buyer didn't just lower the offer, they said "no deal." They had identified many of the same Strategic Value issues we had identified, but they found one that killed the deal. That one was Ted's role and importance in the business. They considered it too risky to purchase a company where the past and the future success was so dependent on just one person, Ted. So, Faraday's $25 million market value dropped to zero on that day.

Once the buyers left the meeting and the shock wore off, Ted looked at me and said he was ready. He was ready to commit to do

Chapter 2: Strategic Value and the Four Pillars

whatever was necessary to build Strategic Value. He set his Strategic Value vision to sell the company in five years for $25,000,000. We jumped in and finished the assessment of his current situation, paying particular attention to what was detracting from his Strategic Value. Then we created a Strategic Value-acceleration plan and began our journey toward his vision. Every part of the company was involved in the process. We upgraded everything from management to administration; we improved systems and processes and adjusted the organizational structure. However, the biggest change was at the top. Ted agreed to replace himself with a CEO from outside the company. Ted then moved into a chief technology role and board chair.

Ted was motivated and committed. We spent three years making good progress on creating the "new and improved" Faraday, focused on his five-year Strategic Value vision. Then I got another call from him. "Joel," he said, "I need to break that promise I made to not consider selling until we had completed our five-year

Strategic Value acceleration plan." He had been approached by another interested buyer, and Ted told them Faraday wasn't for sale. The buyer's response was, "everything is for sale, just name your price."

Ted ended up selling his company. He sold it for nearly three times the lost $25 million offer. He went from a lost opportunity to receiving $70 million in just three and a half years. He had increased Faraday's Strategic Value to become a true "Gotta Have" business. A business that this buyer was willing to pay an unheard of multiple of EBITDA to acquire.

So, What Creates Strategic Value?

When I tell stories like these, with such happy endings, I then hear, "I want a happy ending like that for my story, how do I get there?" My answer is by maximizing your company's Strategic Value. Of course, the next question is, "How do I do that?"

I shared stories of two very successful companies. We all know of some really great

Chapter 2: Strategic Value and the Four Pillars

companies and we all know some that are mediocre at best. What is the difference? Take a buyer's perspective. Why would you buy or not buy those companies? Now be honest, would you buy your company? Better yet, ask yourself if you would pay a premium for your company? If your answer is no, then you know you need to work on your Strategic Value.

So, what is Strategic Value? It's what would make you answer, "Yes, I would definitely pay a premium for my company." Unfortunately, you can't flip a switch or make a couple adjustments to create Strategic Value. It's not complicated, but it's not just one thing. It's a number of things that make up Strategic Value and together create a great company that stands out in the crowd. Each of these things contribute to building your company's Strategic Value. Each are important in themselves, but it's only when there's strength in many things that a company becomes a "Gotta Have."

So now, what are these things? They're everything that makes your business work, including your team, your product or service, your operating practices, your culture, your industry, and your profitability. They're the Components of Strategic Value. To simplify, I've grouped all these Components of Strategic Value into one of four categories that I call the Four Pillars:

Financial
Strategic
Operational
Industry

Think of them as the legs of a table. The legs support the tabletop. If the legs aren't all the same strength, the table will be unstable. As Ted found out, the lack of strength in just one pillar seriously hurt Faraday's Strategic Value.

To further help in assessing the components of value in your company, you can group them into categories within the Four Pillars. Each of the pillars have three or four categories.

Chapter 2: Strategic Value and the Four Pillars

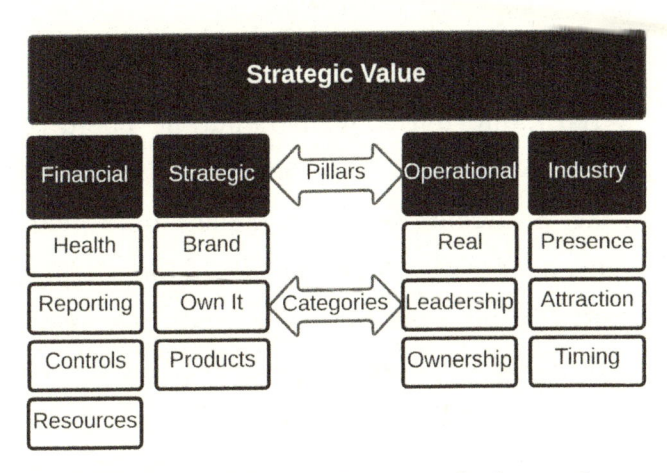

Strategic Value				
Financial	Strategic	Pillars	Operational	Industry
Health	Brand		Real	Presence
Reporting	Own It	Categories	Leadership	Attraction
Controls	Products		Ownership	Timing
Resources				

Chapters 5, 6, 7, and 8 are each devoted to a single pillar with details of the categories and components of value within each pillar.

Strategic Value Anytime

Building strong Strategic Value in your company is a good idea anytime. It does not matter what stage of growth or life cycle your company is in. It doesn't matter what the current or projected economic climate is. **It is always the right time to be building Strategic Value.**

It's not a question of whether strong Strategic Value will pay off. It's a question of how and when it will prove to be the most important thing you, as CVO, did for yourself, your business, and your stakeholders.

Ted came out a winner, but he could've gained even more. The benefits of creating strong Strategic Value are much more than simply a large sale price. Had Ted done what he eventually did when we first started working on his business, he could've reaped the benefits for years before the eventual sale of his company. It's like fixing up your house just to sell it. Sure, you will get a higher price, but the buyer gets to take advantage of that nice new kitchen while you lived for years with the outdated one.

CHAPTER 3: WHY ITS ALWAYS THE RIGHT TIME

Someone's sitting in the shade today because someone planted a tree a long time ago.

Warren Buffet

Strategic Value Made Them Rethink Their Plan

The referral came from an attorney who had been a long-time believer in our firm. His client he said, was a large single location but very successful, specialized auto parts retailer. It was owned by two partners who wanted to sell their business. We set up our first meeting to explore what we could do for them. We didn't know what to expect when we arrived at Tacano's (name has been changed to protect privacy) for the meeting.

What we found was a somewhat run-down building in an older commercial section of town. That fact wasn't surprising, nor that the parking lot was full; however, the street was also lined with customer cars. That was surprising.

They certainly knew their customer base and catered to them. Because of that, they had an amazing customer following. Their volume for a single store was off the charts. At that first meeting we learned that one partner was in charge of the retail operation while the other handled buying and managing the inventory as well as the administrative responsibilities. Not only what merchandise they purchased but how they purchased it was part of their secret to success.

They had both worked hard to build a thriving business that was unique in its industry. Despite having only one store, they successfully competed with some large national chains.

Chapter 3: Why Its Always the Right Time

They told us they were tired and felt it was time to sell. Like so many other companies, because of their operating model and because of the partners' hard work and daily involvement, they were making a lot of money. But they hadn't built much Strategic Value. They weren't a "Gotta Have" at this point.

Their financials amazed us. We had never seen revenue and profits that high from a single store retailer. They had an expectation for a sale price that they shared with us. That initial meeting gave us enough information to know that it was unrealistic to think that a buyer would pay the premium they wanted for the company. Two issues stood out: One was the uniqueness of the business. The other was that both partners, who were critical to the day-to-day operations of the business, wanted to leave the company as soon as possible after a sale.

It took a couple more meetings, but we convinced them to hold off going to market and instead focus on accelerating their Strategic Value.

The first thing we had to overcome was their resistance to making investments into the infrastructure to create future value at the expense of current profits. Then we had to convince them that, like Ted, they would never get their expected sale price unless they reduced the company's dependency on the two of them. They reluctantly agreed to the plan. Changing their perspective took a little time as it usually does. They eventually agreed to hire a younger but experienced manager who understood their market niche. He took over managing day-to-day operations. Then they hired an experienced supply-chain person to be trained by the one partner.

Now, fast forward one year to a meeting we had with them to discuss putting the company on the market. "Why should we sell now?" they both said. "We are working three or less days a week. Mike, our new manager, has basically taken over day-to-day management from us and has implemented new systems and processes, Debbie is now handling most of the buying and inventory. Our efficiency increases have paid

Chapter 3: Why Its Always the Right Time

for our increased management payroll. We have more customer capacity and we are making more money than we ever have. We are going to let it ride for another few years then decide."

Our client had the aha moment many others have had. You don't build Strategic Value and create a "Gotta Have" just to sell a business— **you do it to create a strong, sustainable company that you can enjoy owning and that provides you options for ownership as well as other valuable benefits.**

Four Benefits of Strategic Value

I must repeat it one more time: now is always the right time to be accelerating Strategic Value. Waiting until right before putting a company on the market is not the right approach. In the investment-banker and business-broker world they often refer to getting a company ready for a sale as "putting lipstick on a pig." That's not what Strategic Value is all about.

It's not about cosmetic improvements to attract buyers. It's about creating great companies with real, not cosmetic, improvements. Strong Strategic Value provides companies and owners many benefits. These four benefits are what I believe convince most people, and hopefully you as well, that accelerating your Strategic Value is what you need to be doing. **You need to be doing it now.**

The following four sections in this chapter address the four benefits of strong Strategic Value.

1—Moves the Multiple Needle

This is what most people think of when first introduced to the concept of Strategic Value. It's the reason the company described at the start of this chapter undertook the process. It moves the multiple used to calculate the enterprise value of the company. The typical method of establishing a price for a business is to multiply your company's weighted average—EBITDA—for the past three years by an industry driven multiple.

Chapter 3: Why Its Always the Right Time

That rule-of-thumb industry multiple for calculating a sale price gets thrown out once you have built your Strategic Value and created a "Gotta Have" business. Like the Waterborne and Faraday examples, the much higher "Gotta Have" multiple comes into play. In effect, you create your own multiple. That's how the owners of those companies got very wealthy.

Even if your company doesn't get all the way to "Gotta Have" status, should you put it on the market, all things being equal, it will net a higher sale price. That's because as you go through the process of increasing Strategic Value, you will eliminate many of the reasons a buyer would discount the price. Your company is in good shape, operating as it should for its size, and you're not critical to its success. Because you have invested in its future, there's little the buyer can pick on to negotiate a lower sale price. You can have a very happy ending to your story as well.

Consistently, even if you're not considering a sale for many years, you should change your perspective from owner to buyer. As I mentioned earlier, you need to be asking yourself, "Would I buy this business? If I was the buyer, what would I use to argue a reduction in the price?" Keeping a buyer's perspective, regularly asking those questions and, most importantly acting on them, will eliminate many of the potential discounts when it's time for you to sell.

I remember when a business owner I know received an initial offer for his business. They went through the typical due-diligence process with the potential buyer. He then listened to the potential buyer as they presented a final offer that was much lower than the original. He listened to the rationale for the large discount and then refused the lower offer. He then spent the next two years addressing each of the discount reasons the buyer gave him. The company went back on the market and it was sold without any major discounts. Like Ted in chapter 2, he waited until he went to sell the business to make the improvements. Had he

Chapter 3: Why Its Always the Right Time

followed the Strategic Value concept, he would have sold it faster and probably at a higher price. Maybe more importantly, he would have received the other benefits of Strategic Value prior to the sale.

2—Improves Operating Results and EBITDA

What this means is that Strategic Value can help you make more money! That's because your strong Strategic Value company just works like it should. Don't tell me that isn't a good thing.

Within each of the pillars of Strategic Value, the focus is on creating a stronger, more efficient, better operating, recognizable company. All of these translate into a smoothly operating organization that can maximize revenue with minimal profit leaks. Your company will have the proper level of processes and systems that will result in improved quality, less rework, and more dollars flowing to the bottom line. All this typically results in satisfied customers who will buy more product.

This was a new one for me. I was approached by an attorney regarding working with them on their foreclosure law firm. Not my typical client but when we were done it proved that Strategic Value can work for nearly every type of business. The firm served banks across the country. It wasn't your typical law firm. The activity level in their offices was something I had never seen in any office of any kind. Files were continually moving across the various attorneys and assistants' desks. They had grown rapidly, and they came to us because they were losing control. Clients were starting to get upset. They were spending money on overtime as the volume increased and their processes couldn't keep up. Lost files and rework were compounding the issue.

Although they came to us because of their process and profitability issues, not to build value, we approached the situation from a Strategic Value perspective. Although a lot of the focus was on their process, many other issues were also addressed. As they implemented the changes intended to increase Strategic Value,

Chapter 3: Why Its Always the Right Time

their operating results and profitability began to dramatically improve. It was helped by their newfound ability to service more clients.

Because we took a Strategic Value approach, they received added benefits. Improvements in other pillars resulted in eliminating dependence on any one partner. That, along with an increase in enterprise value, enabled partners to retire if they wished without damaging the firm and at a higher buy out value.

3—Creates Owner Options

Like the partners in the single store, Tacano's, discussed earlier, as the owner of a company with strong Strategic Value, you have multiple options for your company and your ownership. The owners of Tacano's opted to stay in the business on a less than full-time basis while maintaining their ownership and their pay checks. They did eventually sell a part ownership in the business to the manager who was essentially running the business. A few years later they sold the entire company to an outside buyer. When they did sell, it was for an amount higher than the partners stated they wanted at our first meeting. They received a "Gotta Have" multiple.

Owners of companies with strong Strategic Value really like this benefit. Think about it, you have a choice. You can choose to stay very involved in your business for as long as you wish or you can stay partially involved. Better yet, once you have created your company's Strategic Value, you can choose to spend months on the beach in Hawaii. It couldn't get any better than that, lying in the sun collecting checks and talking to your leadership team members just to check in. If that's not your cup of tea, you can simply sell all or part of the business. You can sell it to outside buyers or to an employee group. You could also choose to sell it or pass it down to the next generation of the family and always at a "Gotta Have" multiple.

You have these options only because you maximized your company's Strategic Value.

Chapter 3: Why Its Always the Right Time

A client of mine owned a long-established manufacturing company in the Midwest. He had taken over the family business many years before and he began growing weary of running the company, the winter weather, and the long commutes. He and his wife wanted to spend extended time down south, in a warmer climate, but they didn't see a clear path to that end. He was realistic. He knew that if he sold the company, he wouldn't get the price he needed.

When we met and discussed his vision, he agreed that the best option was to work on accelerating the company's Strategic Value. Within two years of beginning the process, he had improved components in all Four Pillars. His Strategic Value was increasing. They were making more money. He had a COO running the business on a daily basis. Despite the resulting increase in enterprise value, increased profitability, and his COO, he kept the company. He bought that place in Florida that his wife and he always wanted. Instead of staying there occasionally, they moved full time to Florida. He returns to visit occasionally and communicates regularly with his COO. He chose Florida. You can choose Hawaii or anyplace else you want. There has been no sale yet, but we know that when he's ready to sell, the company will be ready and he'll maximize the multiple.

4—Value Insurance

The final benefit is very important but something that you probably don't think of very often if at all. Some owners don't even want to discuss this. Maybe you're different, but I've found most owners who are successfully running their companies don't think about the "what if" scenario. They don't want to think what might happen to the company, their employees, and their families should they and a truck unfortunately meet head-to-head.

Ask yourself, as owner of your company, if you're essentially the company. Are you so important to the company that it would have a hard time surviving without you? If you answered with a yes, the value of your company will drop immediately should you meet that truck. The day after the tragic event, your heirs'

Chapter 3: Why Its Always the Right Time

phone will begin to ring with potential buyers. The buyers will attempt to purchase your business, the one you worked and sacrificed so hard to build, at a bargain price. Your heirs may not have a choice.

However, if you have built strong Strategic Value, everyone will miss you but your company will continue to operate. The value of the company will be maintained. Your heirs can then take their time to make a decision. Your company is operating as a "real" company with a life of its own. Your heirs, because of the Strategic Value you built, will have the benefit of options. They can sell it, or they can decide to keep it with a family or nonfamily leader. Strategic Value enables them to not have to make a quick decision that they may end up regretting. Maybe they will decide to just lie on the beach and collect checks.

CHAPTER 4: STRATEGIC VALUE ACCELERATION

> The way to get started is to stop talking and start doing.
>
> Walt Disney

The Process

Hopefully by now, you have decided that you're going for the "Gotta Have." I'm obviously biased, but you won't regret it. So, you should now be asking, "Okay, Joel, how can I get this done?" Well, in this chapter we will begin the how of accelerating your Strategic Value. As CVO, strengthening Strategic Value is your number one job, and the Strategic Value

Chapter 4: Strategic Value Acceleration

Acceleration Process can be your number one tool to make that happen.

My firm was once engaged by a group who had recently purchased a company. Once they bought it, they hired a new CEO to run it. It was a long-established company that under its former CEO and ownership had become "tired." The new owners saw it as an opportunity to renew the company's place as a leader in its industry and make a lot of money. They committed to making that transition by accelerating the company's Strategic Value. They were focused on making the company a "Gotta Have." Throughout this chapter and in other points in this book, I will refer to this company, Lights Out Products (name has been changed to protect privacy), as an example to illustrate how they did it and how you can do it as well.

Phase 0—Communication

The initial phase that I refer to as phase 0 is the basis for a successful process. You're reading the book. You understand what you want to achieve and why. You're motivated and committed. Your team didn't read the book; they've no idea what Strategic Value is and why you would want it accelerated. If you want them to buy-in and be as motivated and committed as you, they need to be educated.

How you complete phase 0 will depend on your organization, its size, and its culture. At Lights Out, the CVO started with his leadership team. We held a few sessions with the team where he and I talked about what Strategic Value is and why it's so important. We also talked through the process they would follow to accomplish the Strategic Value acceleration. These sessions provided an opportunity for the leadership team to help design the process. This book wasn't available for those sessions, but now that it is, you may want your team to read this book as part of the communication process.

Once the leadership team sessions were completed, the message was communicated to the rest of the company. They made sure that the rest of the company team members

Chapter 4: Strategic Value Acceleration

understood the what, why, and how of Strategic Value creation and a "Gotta Have" business.

Regular communication to the leadership team and the company is very critical throughout every phase of the process.

Phase 1—Assessment

Phase 1 of the Strategic Value Acceleration Process is the assessment. No process works without a starting point, and phase 1 is designed to be that point. You would certainly question your doctor if she prescribed a cure for you without first doing a thorough examination. By the same token, as CVO, you cannot prescribe a path to greater Strategic Value without first completing a thorough assessment. Your doctor, based on symptoms, has some idea of what your problems are. You live and breathe your company, so you probably have a good idea of where your company is today. I'm sure you also know what is and what isn't working. Like the doctor, you can take that as the starting point and build the assessment from there.

Since the rest of the acceleration process is built on the assessment, it's critical that it be totally unbiased and honest. Often CVO's are not intentionally biased in their assessments, it's simply that they may not have anything to compare it to. From their perspective, other than the obvious, it's often hard to see what may be hindering the growth of Strategic Value. If you don't believe that you and your leadership team can perform an unbiased assessment, consider some help from an outside advisor. Also, including employees other than your leadership team in the assessment is always a good idea.

At Lights Out Products, the Strategic Value assessment process was led by the new CEO/CVO. Because he was new to the company, it was easier for him to provide a fresh unbiased look. I worked with him as he led his then current leadership team though the assessment process. Every aspect within every pillar of Strategic Value was assessed, and it was successful in providing a complete picture of their current situation.

Chapter 4: Strategic Value Acceleration

Also, his leadership team and others from the company greatly contributed to and improved the quality of the assessment. It also created a stronger overall buy-in of the process. In addition, it enabled him to assess firsthand, which is a very important component of Strategic Value, the leadership team itself.

The results of the assessment confirmed our early thoughts. The company hadn't reinvested sufficiently in the business or its products. There was a real question of sustainability. Prior ownership had focused for too long on short-term profits and distributions at the expense of long-term growth and value. The picture that the assessment painted was that the lights were going out at Lights Out Products. The commitment to strengthen Strategic Value was what turned the tide in the company.

Chapters 5, 6, 7, and 8 are devoted to the Four Pillars of Strategic Value, defining the various factors within each pillar that create Strategic Value. The assessment process needs to examine each of those factors.

As with phase 0, how you complete your assessment depends on your organization, its size, and its culture. There's no right or wrong way to do it. There's just one requirement: be totally honest and unbiased.

Let's use Lights Out Products to illustrate one successful approach. They began with the CVO Strategic Value online assessment (see our website) to get an initial look at the company's situation. That provided them with some indications of where their focus should be. The leadership team then, by applying the results of the online assessment and the Strategic Value discussions in phase 0, began a series of work sessions. Each session was led by the CVO and focused on some of the categories of each of the Four Pillars. Some categories, such as evaluation of the leadership team and ownership roles, aren't always appropriate for a full team assessment. At Lights Out, the CVO and I held separate sessions to assess those components.

If your organization isn't structured to enable you to conduct the assessment like

Chapter 4: Strategic Value Acceleration

Lights Out did, modify who's included in the process. The more of your team you involve in the process at the appropriate times, the greater the buy-in and the better the results.

Phase 2—Vision

Think of the process of Accelerating Strategic Value as a road trip. In phase 3 you will actually plot out the roadmap. But you need two things before you can do that. You need to know where you are now and where you want to go. Phase 1, the assessment, is intended to provide the starting point. Phase 2 will provide the destination. This is the Strategic Value vision.

It should not be confused with what you probably know as a vision statement. A vision statement is typically more visceral or emotional. Google's vision statement, for example, is "to provide access to the world's information in one click." I encourage you as CEO to go through the process of developing mission and vision statements, as well as core values.

However, this is a different exercise. This is defining where you want the company to be, the destination, at the end of your Strategic Value acceleration journey. Think of the visions already discussed in this book: Waterborne's "$100 million revenue in ten years" vision and Ted's "$25 million sale in five years" vision. This vision is an objective goal, that can be measured. The metrics related to achieving that goal can be defined and monitored.

If your situation is like Lights Out, where you as the CEO/CVO aren't an owner, creating the vision may be a little more complex. At Lights Out, the CEO/CVO utilized a series of planning sessions with the owners to establish an agreed upon Strategic Value vision. In developing this vision, it was decided that because the company needed much "repair work" to ensure its sustainability and future, the vision was based more on improving the company and its performance than specific revenue numbers. The vision included regaining the company's place as a leader in the industry, changing the culture of the company to be a great place to work, and creating a sustainable and valuable company. They simply focused on maximizing Strategic Value and creating a "Gotta Have" business within a five-year window.

While developing your vision, you may also find it a perfect time to define the business or niche your company is or will be in. Once documented in the vision, it will provide you with a reference point when making certain decisions on the roadmap. I've always found that if you can define your business and narrow your niche, you can be more focused and increase your success in maximizing Strategic Value. As explained in chapter 8, the strength of the Industry Pillar is often dependent on what industry and what niche of that industry your company is in.

Phase 3—Roadmap

Now it's time to draw the map and determine the route to your Strategic Value vison.

You and your team can now determine how you will get from where the assessment says you are today to where the vision says you want to go. At the sake of dating myself, it's like when I was growing up and I went with my dad to the AAA office to have them prepare one of their TripTiks for our summer family trip. It showed the route AAA suggested to get from Cleveland to wherever we were heading that year. Then they would stamp warnings onto the map for construction zones and for "speed traps," as well as places of interest along the way. The Strategic Value-acceleration roadmap is your TripTik. Like they did, you need to mark areas on your roadmap that may slow you down or be the most challenging.

In most situations, there are an overwhelming number of things that need to be accomplished along the road from where you are to where you want to be. Although there's not one way to attack them, I've seen the best results by following these steps:

Chapter 4: Strategic Value Acceleration

1. For each pillar list everything that would or could be done to maximize Strategic Value.

2. Again, for each pillar, group those things identified into project categories. Then break the project categories into smaller shorter-term projects.

   For example, at Lights Out, they had identified changing the market's perception of their products, establishing more differentiation for their products and renewing brand recognition. These were consolidated, as were a few more, into an overall project category named "Differentiation." That large category was then broken into shorter, more manageable projects.

3. Despite the importance of the Strategic Value Acceleration Process, your company has limited resources in both personnel and money to apply to the roadmap. You're probably thinking the same thing

clients have told me more than once, "Joel, we still have to do our day job." Therefore, prioritization becomes essential.

In most cases, I suggest choosing no more than three major projects at any one time. I've seen situations where companies identified projects but didn't prioritize or pick three. Then, I would come back for a follow up and status session months later only to find that they were overwhelmed. Nothing got accomplished. They were like deer in the headlights, wondering where to begin. So, the key is to keep it manageable. Everyone wants to make it happen fast, but the best results come from slow and steady—eating the elephant one bite at a time.

Phase 4—Implementation and Monitoring

At this point your destination is defined in the vision, and you have a prioritized roadmap to get there. Now it's time to make it happen. Again, there is not one way to proceed. How you undertake this depends on your company's

Chapter 4: Strategic Value Acceleration

culture and abilities. One method that I've seen work is to assign responsibility for each of the active projects to a team leader, along with an appropriate team, timeline, and budget. This and a reporting and monitoring program keeps the projects on target.

At Lights Out, members of the leadership team were assigned to be project-category leads. They developed the overall category plans and then in turn assigned project leads for the actual defined projects. The project leads put teams together to develop and implement specific project plans. Every team was also responsible for developing a set of metrics to monitor progress. The project leads reported progress weekly on those metrics to the leadership team member. The leadership team member then reported their category progress, metrics, and status at the weekly leadership team meeting. The CFO was given the responsibility for overall monitoring of progress and metrics.

Over the next five years, they methodically worked on the projects and plans to increase

Strategic Value. As they progressed on the roadmap and as was predicted, EBITDA was temporarily reduced as they made the much-needed infrastructure investments. However, as sales and operating efficiency increased, margins and profitability also increased.

At the end of those five years, the company was totally different than it was when the process began. It had reestablished itself as the leader in its industry. It had become sustainable with new technology-based products, efficient operating processes, a great leadership team, and excited, positive employees. It had greatly accelerated its Strategic Value and accomplished its Strategic Value vision. The owners now had a "Gotta Have" business. They had reestablished their reputation and the industry was taking notice.

CHAPTER 5: PILLAR NUMBER 1—FINANCIAL

Price is what you pay. Value is what you get.

Warren Buffet

It's about More Than Just the Money

The Financial Pillar is the first of the Four Pillars that support Strategic Value. I made it first because it's the first thing most people think about when they think value. It's important, but remember, it takes the strength of all Four Pillars to maximize Strategic Value.

The core strategy of the Financial Pillar is **Consistency and Improvement**. That means that your Strategic Value depends on the components of this pillar having predictable processes and continuously improving.

The pillar is typically centered around the CFO or controller function in the organization. However, its more than simply revenue, expense, and profits. I've also included tracking, monitoring, and measurement practices, as well as both internal and external resources. Like each of the pillars, it's broken down into categories. Specific components in each contribute to or detract from Strategic Value.

Revenue, Profits, EBITDA, and Overall Company Health

This category is what typically comes to mind when people think of enterprise value. The components are the basics and are important to Strategic Value. Historic numbers over a trailing five-year period, current numbers, and projected three-year numbers in this category all play a role in evaluating and creating Strategic Value. The assessment provides opportunities for you to look for trends in five years of company

Chapter 5: Pillar Number 1—Financial

sales, revenue, gross profit, and net operating profit. It can provide you with a picture of the company's growth path.

The finer the results can be broken down, the better the assessment. A thorough assessment will include the sources of revenue as well as profitability by type of product or business unit. Recently I saw the financial assessment of a company that had multiple business units. Overall, the assessment indicated very sporadic growth and profit trends over a five-year period. Since there was no business unit breakdown it was impossible to pinpoint what was causing the uncertainly of results. Without that breakdown, it would be nearly impossible to develop an effective roadmap.

I'm sure this next statement isn't going to be a shock to you: Strategic Value increases if revenue and profits continually increase. However, don't get too comfortable, because remember, Strategic Value is based more on future value than current profits.

So, what is more important to accelerating your Strategic Value? It's developing projections for the next three to five years. These projections need to include necessary infrastructure investments and the resulting growth in revenue and profits. Then most important to Strategic Value is meeting those projections.

Other important components in this category include pricing flexibility, cash flow, and company health and resilience. These components play a major role in your company's ability to weather economic or industry turbulence. If your company's product or service pricing is experiencing strong downward pressures or is limited due to your product being considered a commodity, it's reducing your Strategic Value. If that's the case, your roadmap should focus on ways to increase product differentiation. Actually, continually seeking opportunities to move away from commodities toward differentiated products should be part of every company's roadmap.

Chapter 5: Pillar Number 1—Financial

Cash flow sufficiency is also a major contributor to Strategic Value. There's a Strategic Value issue if there's no focus on cash flow or, worse, no ability to measure and predict it. Cash flow is often more important to Strategic Value than profitability. Cash flow projections are an indicator of a "real" company with sound financial management.

Cash reserves and debt levels play a big part in your company's overall health and resilience. Well-funded cash reserves and little debt does increase your Strategic Value. It places you in a position to better survive an economic crisis. It also puts you in a good position to invest in what is needed to strengthen the other Strategic Value pillars.

At Lights Out, the new owners had to invest new funds into the company. They learned that prior ownership not only failed to invest in the future of the company but drained cash out of the company. Without the new funds, should the economy have contracted causing sales to decrease rapidly, the company could've had major sustainability problems.

Financial Tracking and Reporting

The ability to measure and report accurate financial results regularly and quickly plays an important role in building Strategic Value. To grow and improve you need an accurate and timely report card. A report card issued more than one to two weeks after the close of a period is of little value in detecting a problem and addressing it.

"Secret" financial statements are also of little use. If you're not sharing financial results with your leadership team, how will you get them to work toward the Strategic Value vision? That applies also to sharing at least a partial version of the results with much of the rest of your team. This can be a difficult transition for some CEOs who have never opened their books to others in the company. Doing so provides a great opportunity to educate the team about what's important to creating Strategic Value, shares progress toward the vision, and gets everyone on the team focused on the prize.

Chapter 5: Pillar Number 1—Financial

With few exceptions, gross margin or contribution margin can be one of the most important measures to monitor. For that reason, the ability to track the actual costs of producing your products or services is another necessity for building strong Strategic Value. Many companies are weak in this area of the Financial Pillar.

Often in those cases, leadership is simply looking at current profitability. They're reluctant to invest in the people or processes required to understand where the profits are coming from. Because of that reluctance they cannot be sure what products or services are adding to or detracting from profitability. Accelerating Strategic Value typically requires an investment here. Like others, it will reduce short term profitability if you have to add additional personnel, but the return on this investment is usually very quick.

The closer you get to considering a sale of your business, the more important audited financial statements become. Because you're building a "Gotta Have" to maximize the sale price, the interested buyers will insist on audited statements. Make finding the "right" outside accountants a part of your acceleration process. Don't wait until you're ready to put the company on the market to add them to your team.

Controls and Measures

I've included performance metrics, monitoring of those metrics, and controls in the Financial Pillar. They're important tools in your acceleration process. There are two keys to making these tools work for you. The first is to be sure to tie your metrics to Strategic Value creation and your vision. The second is to actually utilize them to drive performance and course corrections. Metrics need to mean something, to be tied to a desired outcome, and to drive performance. Metrics for the sake of metrics don't create Strategic Value.

The establishment of relevant performance metrics and then building them into the culture of the organization can help immensely in your

Chapter 5: Pillar Number 1—Financial

drive to strengthen Strategic Value. I admit, I've no research-based statistics I can point to (although there are probably some) that prove that the establishment and use of metrics increases company success. However, if your experience is the same as mine, I'm sure you will agree that it's true.

There are certain basic financial metrics, such as revenue growth, contribution margin, inventory turns, and many others, that are well known to most leaders. They're important to managing a growing business. To truly drive Strategic Value, though, you need metrics that are developed within the company and specifically designed to move the company toward its Strategic Value vision and goals. Metrics can also be related to specific value acceleration projects.

Lights Out, on their acceleration roadmap, had an important project to strengthen an important competency of the company. After developing their project plan, they established three metrics that related directly to the expected results of the project. These outcome-based metrics included manufacturing yield, turnaround time, and unit cost. The project did result in significant improvements in all three metrics. However, the metrics served even a greater purpose. They made it clear to every team member in the department how they could help increase the company's Strategic Value.

My recommendation is for you to establish a formal process for setting metrics, reviewing performance against those metrics, and responding to that performance. That process will help drive your increased Strategic Value.

Resources

Strategic Value relies on you having the appropriate resources available to do what needs to be done. It's no different for the financial function. Actually, some could argue its most important here. If you're growing your company and at the same time working to create Strategic Value, you need financial leadership with the right experience and skill set. Then you need to provide the appropriate systems, tools,

Chapter 5: Pillar Number 1—Financial

and support.

I worked with a manufacturing company that had grown considerably over an eight- to ten-year period prior to its sale. It was now under the leadership of a new CEO/owner. His CFO had joined the company under the prior owner when the company was smaller.

I was involved with the new CEO/owner as he began his Strategic Value acceleration process. During the assessment, I talked to the CFO and learned that he ran the accounting area with two bookkeeper-level people and another person reporting to him; she spent half her time doing payroll and acting as the HR person and the other half doing accounting tasks. The CFO also oversaw the IT function in the company where he had two employees. What I didn't learn until later was that he also was the go-to person for maintenance, security, and anything else that no one took responsibility for.

When he was hired, he fit well. He enjoyed being an important cog in the company wheel. He may have been the right resource at one time but he wasn't right for where the new CEO/owners wanted to take his company. Within a short time, it became obvious that HR, IT, and maintenance didn't belong under him. Once the organization was restructured and those functions were reassigned, the shortcomings in his accounting skills became more obvious. A new CFO was hired who was a better match for the goal of growing Strategic Value. The change proved to be best for both the prior CFO and the company.

I've also included outside advisors as resources within the Financial Pillar. That could include your attorneys, CPAs, bankers, financial advisors, and business advisors. Having a strong outside team that understands the Strategic Value vision and can work together to help guide and support company leadership, adds another dimension to helping accelerate value.

CHAPTER 6: PILLAR NUMBER 2—STRATEGIC

A brand for a company is like a reputation for a person. You earn reputation by trying to do hard things well.

Jeff Bezos

Strong and Unique

The second pillar is the Strategic Pillar. The core strategy of this pillar is **Strengths and Uniqueness** and applies to products, processes, markets, and business practices. What this core strategy should be telling you is that Strategic Value is created when companies make or do something that's stronger or more unique than the competition. The more difficult it would be for a competitor to catch up, the greater the contribution to Strategic Value. In some cases, if your product or process really stands out, it can actually become the primary driver of Strategic Value. This happened to CleanCo (not their real name) in the following example.

CleanCo was in the commercial janitorial business. They were contracted by customers to clean office and industrial buildings. The industry isn't very glamorous. Companies in this business weren't then nor are they today creating cultures that attract motivated employees. At the time I was working with CleanCo, annual employee turnover in the industry was approaching 400 percent. Not a great testament to the industry and a real negative to their customers who desired some level of consistency.

CleanCo, as part of its process for accelerating its Strategic Value, identified turnover as something that, if they could improve it, would differentiate them and greatly

Chapter 6: Pillar Number 2—Strategic

enhance Strategic Value. So they made reducing employee turnover a top-priority project on their acceleration roadmap. Their approach was to utilize a "career path" concept. They implemented a unique training and certification process. Employees could now see a reason to stay at CleanCo and a way to become certified specialists, supervisors, and even managers. Turnover dropped significantly. It was less than 30 percent of the industry average. The immediate results were improved operating profits and new customers who appreciated more stable and more committed and productive crews.

CleanCo made a considerable investment in time and money to develop their employee program. They believed that the resulting increase in Strategic Value would be worth it. That assumption was soon realized when the CEO/CVO received and, ultimately, accepted an offer from a large out of state competitor to buy his company. The buyer sought them specifically for their employee program. They saw the benefits and they wanted it for their operation. They also knew that by purchasing my client's company they would have it much faster and with less risk than attempting to duplicate it themselves. It was a win-win. My client, who had not planned on selling, received a much higher sale price than was the norm for the janitorial industry, and the buyer received the competitive edge he was seeking.

Brand

The first category within the Strategic Pillar is Brand. Think of what someone thinks of when they hear your company's name—that's your brand. What's the market's perception of your products and services? Do customers think quality and value leader when they hear your company's name? Do they perceive your products and services as being different enough to seek your company out and pay a premium to get them?

Remember Lights Out Products. They were seeking to regain their place as industry leader. The company had that leader reputation for many years. Like the old story that you would

Chapter 6: Pillar Number 2—Strategic

be safe and not be fired for specifying IBM, engineers at customer companies felt the same with Lights Out Products. It was a safe bet to specify them because those engineers knew they would get a product that worked well. They were willing to pay a price that was higher than the competition.

As years went by at Lights Out and leadership didn't invest in new product innovations or new manufacturing techniques, the company's reputation started to suffer. Young engineers at customer companies, those without any history using the products, had no basis for thinking positively about the company's products. That opened the market to newer more innovative companies to take market share. It was obvious: to have any chance of becoming a "Gotta Have," their strong brand had to be reestablished.

Lights Out had to regain the market's perception of the company as an innovative market leader. This became a core component for the roadmap to accelerating their Strategic Value.

They committed to developing new products with new technology and fresh new names. In doing so, they made sizable investments in the future of the company. As expected, these investments were detrimental to current profitability, but future ROI proved the investments were worth the short-term dip in profits. Expectations were that the investments would result in increased sales of new products. More importantly, the new products would change the market's perception of the company and greatly accelerate the company's Strategic Value . . . and it did!

"You Own It"

This category speaks for itself. If you can own something that no other company has, it really drives your Strategic Value. This could be a patent or other intellectual property that you have that makes your product or service better or different. Sometimes it's not your product or service but rather a proprietary process or system that sets you apart (like with CleanCo). The stronger and more unique that thing you own, the more it will add to your Strategic

Chapter 6: Pillar Number 2—Strategic Value.

A regional specialty-construction company gained considerable Strategic Value by owning the rights to a unique concrete-construction method. When engineers had to specify a solution to a particular issue, their proprietary method was often the preferred choice and typically the only choice. Their marketing approach was to raise awareness of their "you own it" with engineering firms. Eventually the word got around, and they went from being just another concrete-construction company to being a unique provider. With that they could better withstand economic downturns (not unusual in their industry), maintain a steady growth rate, and truly accelerate their Strategic Value in what's typically a commodity business.

"You own it" advantages can also come from long-term agreements or contracts. If you can get agreements with customers that will provide a long-term income stream and keep your competition at bay, up goes your Strategic Value. Should you decide to sell the business, these long-term contracts greatly cut down on any discounting based on income risk.

Products, Services, and Customers

This final category within the Strategic Pillar has several components. It's primarily focused on the strength, sustainability, scalability, and concentration of your products and your customers. Strategic Value increases when you have products and customers that are in for the long haul, create the least risk, and have the greatest growth opportunities.

How often do customers purchase your products or services, or both? Can they buy once and then not again for years or are your products something that your customers need to buy regularly? Your Strategic Value will increase if you can create recurring revenue. However, many companies have products or services that aren't bought on a regular basis; it could be just the type of product you sell. Maybe your products are so durable that customers just keep using them without any need to replace them.

Chapter 6: Pillar Number 2—Strategic

Think of a roofing company. Roofing materials are designed to last twenty years or more. Assuming they're installed correctly, the roofing company may have to wait years, if ever, to hear from a customer again. However, if you're creative and innovative, you might be able to create recurring revenue. If the roofing company, for example, created some type of annual service contract that includes inspection, resealing of skylights and chimneys, and perhaps gutter cleaning, they could create recurring revenue. That would not only increase Strategic Value but also cut down on owner stress over cash flow.

The CEO/CVO at Lights Out Products soon realized that their company had a catch-22: they made strong durable products that lasted for years. Like with roofing, a customer could buy one, love it, but not need to ever replace it or buy another. Understanding that even creating new and innovative products would not help the recurring revenue issue, they needed to find another solution.

The company always provided an adjustment and repair service for their customers but had never promoted it or made it a core part of the business. They made investing in and building the service business a key part of their acceleration roadmap for Strategic Value.

Their projections indicated a large potential income stream with a very respectable gross margin. As the CEO/CVO told me, it was "kind of a no-brainer." Within a year, the services area needed to be expanded to enable it to handle the increased volume. Creative marketing efforts were driving more and more service business, more recurring revenue, more dollars to the bottom line, and more Strategic Value to the company. They identified a Strategic Value weakness during the assessment: a lack of recurring revenue. Then they turned that weakness into an accelerator by making it a part of the acceleration roadmap, focusing on it, utilizing a little creativity, and investing in it.

Chapter 6: Pillar Number 2—Strategic

Customer, market, or industry concentrations are another issue that can affect Strategic Value. I'm sure you know of companies that have grown due to one or two key customers. In some cases, they comprise 80 percent or more of the total revenue. Concentration like that creates risk and risk reduces Strategic Value. I would seldom recommend not taking new orders from the company or industry creating the concentration. I would rather see them build diversification into their acceleration roadmap.

I worked with numerous companies that had built strong dependencies on the oil and gas industry during the oil boom beginning in the early 2000s up until its crash in 2014 and 2015. In many of those companies, leadership's thinking was "we are doing great today." They were not thinking of the future and of creating long-term Strategic Value, so there was little incentive to diversify. Many were making a lot of money and not thinking too far into the future. Then in 2015, some of these companies lost as much as 75 percent of their revenue within just a few months. Some worked hard and recovered while for some others, their efforts were too little, too late. They ended up going out of business.

Strategic Value driven management keeps things like customer or industry concentration front of mind. Once identified in your Strategic Value acceleration assessment and included in your acceleration roadmap, fixing it becomes a prioritized project. With you and your team behind it, it's no longer something that can be easily ignored.

CHAPTER 7: PILLAR NUMBER 3—OPERATIONAL

If you are not willing to risk the usual, you will have to settle for the ordinary

Jim Rohn

Sustainability

One of the primary accelerators of Strategic Value is your company's sustainability. The more sustainable, the higher its Strategic Value. Since so much of the Operational Pillar of Strategic Value can directly affect the sustainability of your company, the core strategy of the pillar is **Sustainability**. All three categories within the Operational Pillar— "real" company practices, leadership, and ownership—are focused on creating long-term growth and sustainability. In this pillar, there's a continuing emphasis on the fact that the more the company operates as a real company, as opposed to a smaller owner-driven company, the greater its sustainability and its Strategic Value.

Two of the stories I told earlier to illustrate points in Strategic Value were tied directly to the Operational Pillar. Tacano's, the specialized niche retailer in chapter 3, brought in some new, young managers and created new systems and processes. The purpose was to reduce the dependence on the owners and solidify the company's sustainability. What I didn't mention was that the owner handling buying and inventory wasn't well. The potential for him having to take extended time off or be completely out of the business was a driver in their desire to sell the company. They understood that this one partner's unique knowledge played a major role in the company's success. Without others to take over, his condition jeopardized the company's long-term sustainability and, of

Chapter 7: Pillar Number 3—Operational

course, its Strategic Value.

When Ted in the story in chapter 2 lost that first deal, it was because of his weaknesses in the Operational Pillar. Strengthening his Operational Pillar played a big part in getting Ted the fantastic deal he ultimately received. Despite his excellent products and overall strength in the Strategic Pillar, it wasn't enough to entice the buyer. It took shoring up the Operational Pillar to make it happen.

The Operational Pillar plays such an important role as a contributor to Strategic Value that I want to share one more example. Our firm was engaged to sell a very profitable Alaska based business. After performing a Strategic Value assessment of Cold Comfort Co., (not their real name) our recommendation to the owners was to not go to market yet. They had some major Strategic Value weaknesses. These were especially evident in the Operational Pillar. We suggested a Strategic Value acceleration process before offering the company for sale.

There were major deficiencies in the caliber of their core-team leadership. That leadership consisted of the children who were now running Cold Comfort Co. Unfortunately, due to the family dynamics, this was one of those rare situations where we couldn't convince them to wait. They insisted on going to market immediately. Against our better judgement, we did what they wished, and the results were what we expected.

Initially, we had some excited interest from potential buyers. However, once they learned more about the company, all except one were no longer interested. The one that was still showing interest, then made a very low offer. All the potential buyers voiced the same concern: "It's a great business; however, Alaska is too far away for us to not have the right team, controls, and processes in place . . . and Cold Comfort Co. doesn't have them." After six months, the family relented. We took the company off the market, created the roadmap, and began accelerating Strategic Value.

Chapter 7: Pillar Number 3—Operational

"Real" Company Practices

You're probably asking what does he mean by "real" company practices. The answer is that I had to find something that was better than saying a company had to "act like an adult" if it wanted to increase its Strategic Value. It means that companies must do what larger, successful, valuable companies do operationally. If they do, they can increase sustainability. They can move the company away from dependence on single individuals. In operating like that, I'm not suggesting that companies take on some of the less desirable practices of large corporations that limit innovation and improvement. I'm simply suggesting that they start acting like sustainable, valuable businesses rather than sole practitioners.

There are a couple of quick checks you can do when you start looking at real company practices. First, ask yourself whether you as CEO/CVO, your leadership team, and others in your company truly understand what the company is. What it stands for and what are its short- and long-term vision and goals.

You don't want to be like the CEO of one of the companies I worked with. They were a unique company with great potential for continued growth. In discussions with the leadership team, I discovered that there wasn't a clear expectation of the direction and goals of the company. I heard from them the same thoughts that I had heard at other companies. The CEO didn't define and share his vision and goals, because doing so would prevent him from chasing, as they called it, "the ooh shiny" opportunities.

He, like so many other entrepreneurial CEOs, as his team put it, "never heard an idea he didn't like." That's a CEO not acting like a CVO. Once they moved into the second phase of their Strategic Value acceleration process, they established their Strategic Value vision. I know the CEO struggled with it (and he's probably still struggling today), but by defining the vision, they now had a destination that everyone in the company understood.

Chapter 7: Pillar Number 3—Operational

Now ask yourself how your company does with planning. If you don't have a set planning process, ask yourself why not. The argument I often hear for not planning is that things are changing so fast that it's no longer worth it. I agree, things are changing rapidly, and the idea of the ten-year plan that companies could develop years ago went the way the sedan is going. But the practice of annually developing detailed one-year and more conceptual three-year plans work. Coupled with defined and shared goals they can truly make a difference in accelerating Strategic Value. Having a plan provides a focus for your team and a basis for developing metrics to measure progress. Your Strategic Value acceleration roadmap provides the basis for your annual plans.

Every company follows some operational processes and procedures. When your company was smaller, the processes were probably taught and then passed down verbally. As your company grows, these same processes need to be standardized and documented. Even more importantly, your employees need to be trained on them and actually follow them. You can help create long term sustainability in your company by building process consistency into your culture. You can strengthen that culture by encouraging suggestions for improving those processes. Single point dependencies are minimized in that culture. Adopting process tools such as Lean and ISO can help create and reinforce the culture.

I was greeted by turmoil when I arrived at a manufacturing-company client meeting one day. I learned quickly of a very important but very upset customer. The customer's order was very late, and it had resulted in shutting down their assembly line. I asked, what I assumed the customer had asked, "Why was it late?" And "Why could they not expedite the order for that very angry customer?" The answer from the production manager, "Frank is the only person who knows how to do what needs to be done on those intricate parts and he is on an extended vacation."

Chapter 7: Pillar Number 3—Operational

That was single-point dependency to the max. The result: a very unhappy customer. The company had processes for manufacturing and assembly, but the culture did nothing to support or enforce them. It also did nothing to ensure a situation like this wouldn't occur.

That event reminded me of another company where a long-tenured assembly person left the company. Her leaving created much angst because she had created her own pack of personal-assembly notes. When she left, years of knowledge went with her. I learned that this was a typical practice in the company since the official process sheets were often out of date and wrong. In both companies, fixing these situations obviously became part of their Strategic Value acceleration roadmap!

Consistent processes certainly create Strategic Value. If you can build unique operational competencies on that, your Strategic Value can quickly accelerate to another level. Whatever your business, creating strong, unique competencies can be one of the best drivers of

Strategic Value. They help differentiate you from others in the industry. Think of CleanCo, the janitorial company, and what having a unique operating competency did for them.

A unique competency can also help you protect the niche you serve in the market. Cold Comfort Co., the Alaskan company, for all its issues with leadership, did have a strong competency that interested all the potential buyers. Their market niche was supplying the oil-and-gas-drilling operations on the North Slope of Alaska with food and provisions for the workers. Their strength was their knowledge of how to efficiently get those needed and sometimes perishable supplies up to the North Slope in both summer and winter through the Alaskan tundra (think Ice Road Truckers). Unfortunately, in their case, this competency wasn't enough to overcome their other Operational Pillar deficiencies—just another example of why all pillars and all aspects of a pillar need to be strengthened to create that "Gotta Have" business.

Chapter 7: Pillar Number 3—Operational

Leadership

If you're still reading this book, you plan on taking the role of CVO seriously. You have probably also accepted the fact that building value will require investment. Throughout the process, you will have to make investment decisions about what to invest in and how much to invest, and when. When making those decisions, there's one place that you can't afford to skimp—when you're building your leadership team and company culture. **Having the right team, organized correctly, within the right culture, and matched to the company's Strategic Value vision can prove to be your single biggest creator of Strategic Value. Your team should be built so that the company can catch up to the team rather than the team catching up to the company.**

Here's the scenario. Someone is available. She's a true "A" player, who has the experience you need, fits into the culture, and could truly help you reach your Strategic Value vision. Unfortunately, she wants $25 thousand more than your target salary. Should you hire her or pass? When you make that decision, think value contribution over her tenure rather than simply her cost today.

When I was building my leadership team as CEO/CVO, I had three objectives: (1) remove those members who were mired in the past, those who were pessimistic about our ability to achieve our Strategic Value vision; (2) replace them with experienced, forward-thinking believers; and (3) adjust the organizational structure to provide the strongest leadership in the areas critical to the Strategic Value vision. Building my team cost us short-term profits as we raised salaries to get the right people and as we added needed new positions. As expected, in the long-term it paid and will continue to pay in value creation.

One more leadership area I want to mention is advisory boards. You and your leadership team are in the forest. A properly constructed advisory board with the right people can provide you with a much different perspective from outside the forest.

Chapter 7: Pillar Number 3—Operational

There are certain elements to creating the right board for your company. Each member should have a purpose. They should possess unique strengths and experiences that can help you in the quest to create Strategic Value. The members must feel that they can say what they're thinking. They cannot be afraid of being removed from the board for disagreeing with you or the team. Diverse thought and input should be sought from the board. If you have never formed or worked with advisory boards, there are organizations who can help you create and manage them.

Ownership

No other factor can affect Strategic Value, both positively and negatively, to the degree that the role of an owner can. As Ted and so many others have learned, **the more important ownership is to the operation of the company, the lower its Strategic Value**. An owner isn't and shouldn't be irrelevant in the company. What hurts Strategic Value is owners who are critical to its future success.

We have all seen companies where an owner is the primary sales contact and has crafted great relationships with most of the customers. We have seen others where the owner is the core talent or the only decision maker.

Sometimes its unintentional. The company grows but the owner has just never delegated responsibilities. In others it's intentional, the owner just doesn't want to delegate. Letting go can be really tough. Some owners like being the core of the company. They don't want to admit that someone else could actually do their job and maybe even do it better than them. Positive things can happen when you do admit it. Waterborne, the company in chapter 1 with a "$100 million in ten years" strategic vision is a great example of this.

In a few of the value-creation stories in this book, an outside CEO was brought in. Please don't assume that this is always the right answer. Most of the time, as the company grows, it's simply a case of an owner creating a leadership team that they trust and can rely on. Then the

Chapter 7: Pillar Number 3—Operational

owner can "let go" and rely on their team for the tasks and decisions they should be responsible for.

One of my favorite "letting go" stories involves the co-owner/CEO of Wyners (not its real name), a multistore retail chain. Marc was a second-generation owner and had watched his dad start and grow the company. When he and his younger brother took over management, they continued the expansion and were now in nearly fifty locations.

It didn't take me long to understand one of Marc's traits. He wanted to be involved in just about every decision, no matter how big or small. If I was with him when he did it, I made it a point to talk to him afterward. "Marc," I would say, "you pay that person too much money for you to be doing his job. If you don't trust him to make the right decision, you should find someone to replace him." I think he finally got so tired of hearing me say it that he started to let go.

One day we were meeting in his office. His large windows provided a nice view of the front parking area and main entrance. There, employees were loading a van with some last-minute merchandise going out to a new store that was opening the next day. Marc sat there fidgeting and looking back and forth between me and the activity outside. Then he turned to me and said, "So, Joel, aren't you proud of me? You know, before I was "cured," I would have left our meeting and gone out there to check what they were putting in that van."

My advice to an owner/CEO is that to be an effective CVO you need to follow the advice of a management book I read many years ago and is still available today. In their book, *Flight of the Buffalo: Soaring to Excellence, Learning to Let Employees Lead*, James A. Belasco and Ralph C. Stayer (1994) explain why you need to lead your company like the lead goose rather than the head buffalo. They say that in a herd of buffalo, if the head buffalo is killed, the rest of the herd stops and waits for the head buffalo to get back up and lead again. They say, instead,

Chapter 7: Pillar Number 3—Operational

if you're the lead goose and you move back in the formation to rest, another goose will move up to lead until you're able to come back to the front.

CHAPTER 8: PILLAR NUMBER 4—INDUSTRY

A ship in the harbor is safe, but that's not what ships are built for.

John A. Shedd

Are You the Best in Your Industry?

The industry your company operates in can have a direct effect on its Strategic Value. What's even more important is your company's position in your industry. The Industry Pillar is divided into three categories: industry presence, industry attractiveness, and timing. The core strategy of the pillar is **Positioning and Visibility**.

Chapter 8: Pillar Number 4—Industry

A CEO once told me that they liked to fly below the radar. In that way, he said, "My competition doesn't target us, and we just exist as a quiet company." They may have been a quiet company, but they weren't a high value company.

As a buyer, why would you want an unknown company? As an employee, what would attract you to work for a quiet company that no one knows about? As a customer, I certainly want to buy from a company that's known and respected in its industry. You can gain credibility and Strategic Value by how you're positioned in your industry.

Freeform Industries (another real story with a made-up name), had been in business since the '50s. Although a technology-based company, it had let its technology development lag. Its competitors were fast approaching and beginning to exceed the technology in Freeform's products. Because they had been the leader in the industry for so long, their historic reputation enabled them to remain one of the best-known brands. Their brand helped them hold their position in the industry and also kept their egos strong.

But there was decay below the surface. Eventually, their reputation in the industry began to slip. They no longer were known as the best company in the industry with the most innovative products. Competitors saw this as the opening they needed to make a strong move toward their customers. Leadership at Freeform woke up and saw what was happening. Their Strategic Value was taking a nosedive, and to stop the slide, they knew that they needed to regain their position in their industry.

They developed a new Strategic Value acceleration roadmap, with industry position as the priority. They accomplished it by refocusing on what made them the best in the past—innovative technology, performance, and customer service. As expected, profits decreased for the short-term, but the results made it well worth it. They regained their leadership position in the industry, customers returned, employee

Chapter 8: Pillar Number 4—Industry

retention increased, employee recruitment was easier, and long-term company Strategic Value was maximized.

Industry Presence

As illustrated with Freeform Industries, your company's visibility within its market and the industry's awareness of the company can play a major role in the Strategic Value of the company. Industry presence is always important, but it's even more so when you're ready to sell a company. Most buyers, at least the ones that you would want to consider, arc (not surprisingly) attracted to the best companies in their industry. They want the "Gotta Have" companies of the industry.

Your best buyer understands that profitability can be increased relatively quickly. However, a poor reputation within your industry can be much more difficult and more expensive to fix. Why build a "Gotta Have" business that no one knows about?

Visibility, standing, and reputation within the industry add Strategic Value in other ways as well. The job of the HR department becomes easier as they attempt to recruit new employees. The marketing department will find that PR opportunities are easier to obtain because of the reputation and awareness of the company by the media. There are three levels of industry standing: (1) not being in the top tier, (2) being *an* industry leader, and (3) actually being *the* industry leader. The Strategic Value of the company takes a sharp increase when you replace *an* with a *the*.

Industry Attractiveness

Sometimes no matter how well your company is known or its status in your industry, the industry itself can limit a company's Strategic Value. Certain industries are simply not attractive to some buyers and to some employees. That could be because of environmental, social, or economic reasons. There are probably very few buyers interested in purchasing your coal company, no matter how much money its making and how strong its

Chapter 8: Pillar Number 4—Industry

Strategic Value pillars are.

Many years ago I worked with a company in the metal plating business. It was a good company with an unattractive but in demand product. New governmental regulations had been instituted to control pollution, and they couldn't afford the cost of upgrading their processes to those regulations. Their only options were to either close down or sell the company. The only interest came from buyers who were already in the industry. The company was sold, but despite their strength in three of the pillars, there wasn't much they could do with the fourth pillar. They ended up nearly giving the company away.

Strategic Value can also be reduced by another factor external to the company: industry risk. If your company supplies the oil-and-gas-drilling industry, you have benefitted from some great years as oil exceeded $100 a barrel. However, you have probably also struggled through some major downturns in the industry. An industry with major fluctuations in demand actually affects two pillars. In the Financial Pillar it affects the core strategy of consistency. In the Industry Pillar it creates industry risk. Not every potential buyer or employee has the stomach for a roller-coaster ride; thus, Strategic Value suffers.

There's not much you can do to change the nature of the industry you're in or you serve. So in many situations, your fix may be diversification. There were many companies who saw their Strategic Value take a hit when the bottom suddenly dropped out from under the oil and gas industry. That also happened to many companies serving portions of the defense industry when spending was being drastically curtailed. They had built their Strategic Value on serving the defense industry only to look toward the prospect of losing much of that value. Some companies serving either of these industries were able to maintain or re-establish lost Strategic Value through diversification. They assessed their competencies and sought out other industries where those competencies could be applied.

Chapter 8: Pillar Number 4—Industry

Diversification can also be achieved through either acquisition or merger. Acquiring or merging with another company serving a different industry can result in a rapid increase in Strategic Value. Acquisitions come with some risk themselves, so although sometimes an excellent solution, they need to be done for the right reasons and done correctly.

If you're in a less attractive or risky industry, don't give up yet. There's another way that you can offset the negative effect it has on your Strategic Value. Go back to the Strategic Pillar and create a "you own it" process, product, or service. Doing that can put you in a lead position in your industry. A "you own it" that no other company in your industry can easily copy can make even a risky industry more attractive and increase your Strategic Value. Think about what happened to CleanCo in a less than glamorous industry.

Timing

Timing comes into play when you consider a sale of your company. Maximizing Strategic Value, as has been seen in some of the examples in this book, can vastly increase the potential sale price of your company. However, there are various external factors that affect the amount potential buyers are willing to offer to purchase even a "Gotta Have" company. The economy, a troubled industry, interest rates, and general uncertainty in the market can all affect what buyers will be willing to pay or how they will try to structure the deal.

The advice that's easy to give but tough to do is to sell your company right before the market peaks. Unfortunately, there are no sure indicators, but Strategic Value helps no matter the outside factors. If you had planned to sell but the economy has gone in the wrong direction, you have options. If you wait to sell until the economy improves, your strong Strategic Value provides a more stable company that can weather tough times and still maintain its value. If you need to sell despite the timing, even in

Chapter 8: Pillar Number 4—Industry

poor markets, some deals do get done. Those are typically companies who have maximized their Strategic Value or, better yet, have become truly "Gotta Have" businesses.

CHAPTER 9:
THE CVO IN FAMILY BUSINESS

> The family serves the business. Neither will do well if the business is run to serve the family.
>
> Peter Drucker

A Possible Hurdle

Being the CVO is never easy. It takes commitment, communication, and courage to maximize Strategic Value. You certainly don't need an additional hurdle, yet certain ownership situations can create just that. Those situations are family-owned and family-run businesses where there are multiple family members involved.

Chapter 9: The CVO in Family Business

If you're in a family-run business, you can probably relate to this story that will illustrate the hurdles. If you're not in a family business, this can apply to partnerships as well.

I was introduced to a family-owned service business that we will refer to as LastDance Services. It was run by two third-generation brothers. The company, under their grandfather and then their father's leadership had built a good reputation and had grown over the years. I was told by the brothers that their goal was to be the leader in their industry. They wanted to continue to grow both organically and through additional acquisitions.

During the initial Strategic Value assessment, I learned that everything wasn't as it appeared. They had a bad case of what afflicts so many family businesses. The two brothers, although totally committed to the company, had very different management philosophies and lifestyles. One brother was more reserved, both in how he managed and how he lived. His lifestyle enabled him to save and invest. His brother, on the other hand, was much more outgoing, both in the business and out of it. He had more expensive tastes and needed to impress. On his salary, his lifestyle didn't enable much, if any saving.

This was certainly not a unique situation in family businesses. On the surface, both partners wanted to grow their company and create value. However, because of their lifestyle choices they had different personal needs. One of the brothers saw no way to stop taking today's profits out of the business. Even the LastDance Services employees saw the conflict. They knew that although the brothers talked about a common Strategic Value vision, there wasn't a common commitment to achieving it.

There were a lot of very difficult meetings and a lot of angst. The one brother finally got it. Slowly, he adjusted his lifestyle, and they were able to reduce the amount of cash going out to the brothers and instead reinvest it into the company. Although their plan was pushed out a couple years, they began to grow and make acquisitions. Today, LastDance Services has reached the brothers' Strategic Value vision and is one of the most successful companies in its industry.

It worked for them, but as I learned in dealing with so many other family businesses, sometimes it just cannot be fixed. The sad news is that so many family-owned businesses and even nonfamily partnerships with great potential to become "Gotta Have" businesses never even come close. They squander a golden opportunity for themselves and for future generations because they just can't get on the same page.

The Silver Bullet

Changing how a family thinks of themselves and their business is the closest thing I've found to a silver bullet for creating "Gotta Have" family businesses. Instead of thinking of the business as a family business, it should be thought of as a business that just happens to be owned by a family. In other words, run the business like a real company. Manage it like a real company.

Make decisions like a real company. The company's Strategic Value depends on it—as does the family's future.

If your family-owned business can create a common Strategic Value vision, they've taken the first major step in operating like a real business and building Strategic Value. However, simply establishing the vision is never enough. Each family member must also understand what it will take to get there. Agreeing that their vision is a "Gotta Have" that will support generations to come is easy. Agreeing that achieving it will require short-term sacrifices is much more difficult.

Whether its siblings in the same generation or it's a parent and their children, getting them to agree on committing to create Strategic Value for tomorrow is difficult. At LastDance, it was two very different brothers. In others, it's two generations in the business with two very different personal horizons. The Easy Shift Company had both.

Chapter 9: The CVO in Family Business

Easy Shift (not its real name) was a family-owned manufacturing company that had multiple generations plus siblings. The cast of characters at Easy Shift included a parent nearing retirement who had become very risk adverse. She didn't want to do anything that could affect her retirement lifestyle. There was a divorced daughter, who relied on her income from the company to support her kids and their private school. Finally, there was the youngest, unmarried son who wanted to grow and create a "Gotta Have" and was willing to invest whatever was needed back into the business.

Due mainly to the drive and leadership of the son, they had built up some strength in each of the pillars. They had good margins. They had products and brands that differentiated the company from the competition and that customers asked for by name. They were leaders in their industry. They had a good team and decent operating processes. Their only barrier to becoming a "Gotta Have" was the family itself.

I was starting to doubt whether I would be able to ever help them. They were each strong willed and set in their positions. Then I suggested an advisory board. They agreed to it, and we were able to put together a strong board with four very experienced outside advisors. It worked for a while. I was actually getting optimistic that we could get this to work. Then, at a heated board meeting when the mother didn't like our Strategic Value recommendations anymore, she disbanded the board and fired us all. I lost touch with them after that, so I'm not sure what happened. I hope they were able to agree on a common vision and roadmap, because they certainly had the potential to become a "Gotta Have" that happened to be owned by a family.

For years I've been told by the leaders of families in business that their focus is on being the steward of the family business and ensuring its success for the long-term. That's exactly what they would be doing by building Strategic Value and creating a "Gotta Have" business.

Family-owned businesses have the same

Chapter 9: The CVO in Family Business

benefits as any closely held business. Unlike a public company, they can invest in their future without worrying about short-term quarterly results. However, to take advantage of that benefit, every family business owner needs to do more than simply agree. They need to commit not only to the vision but to the Strategic Value roadmap that will get them there.

Some family members may not be able to commit to investing in the future. If they're dependent on short-term profit distributions, it may be time for that family member or the rest of the family to make a choice. There are only a few options. The worst thing they could do is nothing. The conflict and resentment would continue without an end. Not only would building Strategic Value become nearly impossible, value would likely decline. The decision is straight forward. Either go for the Strategic Value vision or halt the quest to build Strategic Value. If the decision is to follow the roadmap and accelerate Strategic Value, family members who can't commit to the journey need to sell their shares and leave the company.

CHAPTER 10: LEADING AS THE CVO

> A leader takes people where they want to go. A great leader takes people where they don't necessarily want to go but ought to be.
>
> Rosalynn Carter

Changing from Advisor Back to Doer

After more years than I care to count spent advising my CEO and owner clients how to become the CVO of their business (and loving most every minute of it), I received an offer too good to pass up. I was offered the opportunity to become the CEO of a client company. I saw it as an opportunity to practice what I was preaching for so many years.

Chapter 10: Leading as the CVO

The company was long established and had been a leader in its industry. Ownership believed, for good reason, that they needed fresh leadership. They understood that the company had lowered a bit over the last several years. From my perspective, it seemed obvious that what they needed was for the new CEO to become the CVO and re-establish their Strategic Value.

That's what I as CVO did for the next few years. My team and I accelerated the company's Strategic Value and focused on making it a "Gotta Have." By moving from advisor to doer I reconfirmed the importance of the CVO's leadership in the process of creating Strategic Value. This chapter is devoted to successful CVO leadership.

Believe in the Role

The first—and maybe the most important—leadership trait for becoming the CVO of your company is to take the role seriously. You must believe in yourself as the CVO. If you do not, how can you expect your leadership team or the rest of the company to follow you?

So, CVO leadership lesson number one is to not just say you're the CVO but totally transform yourself into that role. You must believe it if you expect your team to believe it. Like any leadership situation, you need to do what you say. If you tell the team you're going to create value by investing in the future, you need to actually invest in the future.

Where are We Going and How Will We Get There?

You have established a Strategic Value acceleration vision for your company. Now as CVO, you need to communicate that vision. The clearer you can communicate that vision the more support, excitement, and "buy-in" you will generate throughout the organization.

Simply stating a Strategic Value vision, however, isn't enough. It's your job as CVO to teach the principles of Strategic Value. Your teams need to understand what builds it, what detracts from it, and why it's so important to your company's future. You know you cannot

Chapter 10: Leading as the CVO

accomplish your plan alone; you need your team's help. For you to succeed, they will need to be as focused as you.

If you communicate Strategic Value until you feel like you just cannot communicate Strategic Value anymore . . . communicate it again. As CVO you can never over communicate Strategic Value.

Hold On Tight and Let It Happen

If you have gotten this far in the book, you know that the basic premise of Strategic Value is to not sacrifice long-term Strategic Value for short-term profitability. Because it's so fundamental to creating Strategic Value, as CVO you must believe in it and commit to it. Your roadmap will include the investments and resources required to achieve your Strategic Value vision and move toward "Gotta Have" status.

The easy part of the ride is developing the plan. You're going to have to hold on tight. Maybe even take a TUMS or two to settle your stomach as you implement the plan and invest real money into building future value. As CVO, you need to believe in yourself, in the concept of Strategic Value, and in the fact that you know what needs to be done to accelerate value. You need to have faith in the ultimate results. It's your commitment to make it happen that will make it happen.

If you're still having doubts about this concept, refer back to the examples of Robert Iger from Disney and Jeff Bezos from Amazon in chapter 1.

Make the Hard Decisions and Get the Right Team

As CVO your success will depend on having the right leadership team members in the right roles. This means the following:

1. Team members who can get on board with what you're attempting to achieve and how you're going to get there.

2. Team members who can handle their leadership roles when you attain your

Chapter 10: Leading as the CVO

Strategic Value vision. You want the company to catch up to the team, not the other way around.

3. Having the positions and people you need to get you to your Strategic Value vision, even if it means waiting on their ROI.

4. Operating in the best organizational structure for what you're attempting to achieve.

These changes may be your first real investment in your infrastructure. You may find that you will have to invest by adding new positions, increasing the level of some positions, and adjusting some salaries. It will likely have an effect on your current profitability, but know that it's what you need to do.

As you make those hard decisions and build the team, don't be surprised by the amount of questioning and concern you may encounter from others in the organization. It will occur despite your explanation of what you're attempting to achieve. It's just not what most people are comfortable with. It goes against what most have been taught. It's also why you need to have the right people on the team.

It Goes Beyond the Leadership Team

The best performing organizations are where all the team members act like owners. Most organizations have some people who behave like owners because its who they are. The majority, however, simply come to do their job and go home—that's not a great environment to maximize Strategic Value. Your job as CVO is to lead the nonowners into becoming owners. It won't happen overnight, but slowly over time with a lot of reinforcement from you and your reconstructed leadership team, attitudes will change. They will begin to act and perform like their name is on the door. Like it was their company. Then they will also become more comfortable suggesting improvements and changes to the way things are done.

People will also take on ownership attitudes the more they know about the company. Begin sharing more information. Hold monthly all

Chapter 10: Leading as the CVO

company meetings where you share financial and performance results, highlight customers, reward exceptional employees, and reinforce your plan and Strategic Value vision.

In my role as CVO, I began a series of programs designed to create a sense of importance and ownership for employees throughout the organization. We had monthly "lunch with the CEO/CVO" sessions with ten different employees from a cross section of the company. Our periodic "have a cup of Joe with Joel" encouraged groups to come and sit with me to discuss what was going on in the company.

My favorite was my next generation Navigators group. It was a select group open to all nonmanager or supervisor team members. There was an annual application process, and only twelve were chosen to be in the group. That group of future company leaders met monthly, toured other companies, addressed certain employee and performance concerns, and then carried the message to the rest of their coworkers. They became owners.

Prioritize the Plan and the Investment

You and your leadership team will probably get excited about the Strategic Value acceleration roadmap and plan when it's developed. What you don't want is to see that excitement wane as implementation stalls. What works in many companies is applying a rule of three. Once the plan is developed, pick the three highest priority areas to work on and invest in. Prioritization criteria can begin with what will create the most value increase. Then you can adjust that priority based on realistic investable resources. Prioritizations will likely shift as the process progresses, but, again, if you limit it to three active major projects, you should be able to stay under control and get them completed.

Always Protect Your Brand

In building a "Gotta Have" your brand is golden. It's a major contributor to Strategic Value. It affects every pillar. Revenue, pricing, profitability, customers, your team, your standing in the industry, and your sustainability

Chapter 10: Leading as the CVO

are all dependent on your brand. It's fragile and once damaged, it's the most difficult of the components of Strategic Value to rebuild.

To protect it, you need to know what it is you're protecting. As CVO your task is to ensure that everyone in and out of the company has a consistent answer to "What do people think of when they hear our company name?" It's up to you and your leadership team to continually reinforce the brand internally. There are also a number of tools available to find out what your customers are thinking.

Be a Great Place to Fail

As Jeff Bezos stated in a 2019 letter to shareholders, "If the size of your failures isn't growing, you're not going to be inventing at a size that can actually move the needle." I know, it's another Jeff Bezos example, but it certainly illustrates the point. He made Amazon into a company where it's safe to fail. In fact, he said that Amazon was the best place to fail.

As CVO you need to take that same attitude. To accelerate your Strategic Value, whatever your company is doing today, it will have to do it differently in the future. It will have to innovate everything it makes and does, every day. **A culture of innovation requires an approval for failure.**

As CVO you may find this culture attitude adjustment is difficult for some members of your team. They may have trouble wrapping their heads around the idea that failure is okay, let alone encouraged. Those may be the same people most likely to utter the ten words that are most effective in stopping the creation of Strategic Value: "but this is the way we have always done it." If those people can't be converted to your innovative culture, they need to find another place to work.

In Robert Iger's book that I referenced earlier, *The Ride of a Lifetime*, he says, "I know why companies fail to innovate, its tradition. Tradition generates so much friction every step of the way." He adds, "Nothing is a sure thing,

Chapter 10: Leading as the CVO

but you need at the very least to be willing to take big risks. You can't have big wins without big risks."

Never Take Your Eye off the Prize

The ultimate result of Strategic Value creation is a "Gotta Have" business. That goal should be your metric. At the end of every week, ask yourself, "Are we any closer to being a true 'Gotta Have'?" and "What can we do next week to keep moving toward that goal?" Be honest and be specific and make it a part of your leadership team meetings to ask that same question. It makes for some great conversation and provides opportunities to ensure the team is on the same page.

As Steven Covey (1989) said in *The 7 Habits of Highly Effective People*, "Begin with the end in mind."

Keep Going

Someone once told me when I joined a Sunday morning bike-riding group, "It's not if you will fall, it's when." Building a "Gotta

Have" is no different. Like anything anyone attempts, there will be setbacks. Some things you try in your quest to build value won't work. As the CVO leader, you just need to admit that something didn't work as planned, regroup, make some adjustments to the plan, and go forward again. You will be teaching your team valuable lessons by your admission and by your persistence.

See It as Half Full

As CVO you must believe that this is all possible. You have to instill in your team the belief in their ability to build that "Gotta Have" business. I, like many of you as entrepreneurial leaders, are optimistic. I believe it's a prerequisite for the job. You need to be optimistic and be able to envision a different and better future if you hope to inspire and motivate your team to work toward that shared Strategic Value "Gotta Have" vision.

Some of you, like myself, have probably been accused at times of being too optimistic. Maybe we are, but that's okay if we remain realistic.

Chapter 10: Leading as the CVO

Realistic optimism can be helpful in your role as CVO. What you can't have on your team is a lot of pessimism. Caution yes, pessimism no. "Chicken Littles" have no place on a team focused on accelerating Strategic Value.

Now, quoting Robert Iger one last time, "Optimism sets a different machine in motion. Especially in difficult moments. . . . This is not saying things are good when they are not and it's not about conveying some innate faith that 'things will work out'. . . it's about believing that you and the people around you can steer toward the best outcome and not communicating the feeling that all is lost if things don't break your way. The tone you set as a leader has an enormous effect on the people around you. **No one wants to follow a pessimist.**"(Emphasis mine).

CONCLUSION

> Fight for the things that you care about but do it in a way that will lead others to join you.
>
> Ruth Bader Ginsburg

My Objectives

I was excited to finally be writing my book and checking it off my bucket list. I wanted to get started, but before I could, my publisher asked me to answer some questions related to what I wanted to accomplish and what I wanted my readers to come away with. He began by making me describe the premise of my book:

> The premise of my book is that the primary job of the CEO or owner of a privately held business needs to be to

Conclusion

serve as the CVO, or Chief Value Officer. In that role, it is their responsibility to accelerate the company's Strategic Value and create a "Gotta Have" business with maximum enterprise value.

He then asked, After someone reads your book, what is the main thing you hope they understand or learned?

I want the reader to understand the following:

- The concept and importance of accelerating Strategic Value
- The Four Pillars of Strategic Value
- The tremendous benefits of creating strong Strategic Value
- The rationale behind always building Strategic Value, whether or not the owner has plans to sell their business
- The importance of the CEO or owner's role as Chief Value Officer (CVO) and how best to succeed in that role.

He also asked what would be a common objection to the recommendations that will be presented in the book:

> The investment and time required to build Strategic Value and the difficulty of that very necessary mind shift from a focus on short-term profitability to long-term value creation.

Finally, he asked what I believed should be three objectives that readers of the book should have related to the contents of the book:

1. Creating a growth-oriented, sustainable company with maximum enterprise value.

2. A strong, profitable company while they own it and the ability to transition out of the company when they choose, receiving a great deal of money.

3. Protecting their company's value over the long-term.

Conclusion

That's what I set out to do in writing this book. I remain committed to these objectives because of their importance to the future of all growing businesses. I hope you feel that I accomplished them. If I did and if you believe in it and commit to it, we could have many more "Gotta Have" businesses. I would encourage you to go to www.ChiefValueOfficers.com, or email me at joelstrom@chiefvalueofficers.com and let me know what you think.

Value Creation Takeaways

As a conclusion to this book, let me leave you with what I would refer to as a few value-creation takeaways.

Commitment

As CEO you obviously have a lot of responsibilities and every day brings new challenges. However, you're the one person in the company that's responsible for creating value. It's your ultimate responsibility and why you need to commit to adding CVO to your title.

Timing

It's always the right time to be accelerating your company's Strategic Value. Do not wait until you're ready to sell the business. The sooner you maximize it, the sooner you and the company can realize the benefits that come with strong Strategic Value.

Four Pillars

The building blocks of Strategic Value can be separated into Four Pillars of value. Each pillar needs to be strengthened to maximize the company's value. One weak pillar will prevent your company from reaching "Gotta Have" status.

A Mind Shift

Accelerating Strategic Value requires that you change from a total focus on profits today to a focus on building value for tomorrow. As CVO you need to have the courage to do that!

Ultimate Reward

When you do sell your company, if you have strengthened your Strategic Value, you can demand a much higher sale price. And if you have created a "Gotta Have" business, one that everyone wants, you can truly exceed all value constraints.

Strategic Value Assessment

As I mentioned in the introduction, the best way to begin your Strategic Value acceleration journey is to take my free online CVO Strategic Value Assessment. After answering questions pertaining to components of the Four Pillars of Strategic Value, you will receive your company's current Strategic Value score and suggestions on how to improve it. Once you have completed the assessment, should you desire, I will schedule a personal, no cost or obligation, discussion to review your score and help you begin your acceleration process.

Access the assessment at
www.ChiefValueOfficers.com.

ABOUT THE AUTHOR

Joel is the founder of Chief Value Officers. His practice is focused on only one thing: helping CEOs accelerate their company's Strategic Value and moving their businesses from ordinary to extraordinary. He developed the concept and process of Strategic Value based on more than four decades of practical experience as a business owner, advisor, investment banker, and CEO. His clients have realized spectacular results when working with Joel and following his value creation methods.

Besides his client successes, he owned and grew his own manufacturing company and founded successful growth and value consulting practices in both Ohio and Arizona. He recently

About the Author

completed a five-year period where he served as the CEO of a technical products manufacturing company. During his tenure as CEO and in his role as CVO, Joel led that organization through a remarkable transformation. Utilizing the concept of Strategic Value, he was able to maximize the enterprise's value and secure its place as a world leader in its industry. Once his mission with that company was complete, he decided to return to his passion of helping clients maximize their Strategic Value by founding Chief Value Officers.

Joel has facilitated CEO peer groups and provides keynote presentations, workshops, and seminars on business growth and value creation to industry organizations and associations across the country. His articles about strategy, growth, and value creation appear regularly in local and national publications. Joel was instrumental in developing and presenting educational programs to help manufacturing companies accelerate their value.

He sits on corporate and advisory boards and is active in civic and industry associations. The Institute of Management Consultants designated Joel as a Certified Management Consultant. He holds a degree in mechanical engineering from Case Institute of Technology and an MBA from the Weatherhead School of Management at Case Western Reserve University.

Made in the USA
Monee, IL
28 April 2021